Treasury of Book Ornament and Decoration

537 Borders, Frames and Spot Illustrations from Early Twentieth-Century Italian Sources

Edited by Carol Belanger Grafton

Dover Publications, Inc., New York

CONTENTS

Published in Canada by General Publishing Company, Ltd., 30 Lesmill Road, Don Mills, Toronto, Ontario.

Published in the United Kingdom by Constable and Company, Ltd., 10 Orange Street, London WC2H 7EG.

Treasury of Book Ornament and Decoration: 537 Borders, Frames and Spot Illustrations from Early Twentieth-Century Italian Sources is a new compilation, first published by Dover Publications, Inc., in 1986. The sources of the pictorial material are indicated in the Publisher's Note. Many items appeared in color in the original, but are reproduced here in black and white.

DOVER *Pictorial Archive* SERIES

Treasury of Book Ornament and Decoration: 537 Borders, Frames and Spot Illustrations from Early Twentieth-Century Italian Sources belongs to the Dover Pictorial Archive Series. Up to ten illustrations may be reproduced on any one project or in any single publication, free and without special permission. Wherever possible, include a credit line indicating the title of this book, editor and publisher. Please address the publisher for permission to make more extensive use of illustrations in this book than that authorized above.
The reproduction of this book in whole is prohibited.

Manufactured in the United States of America
Dover Publications, Inc., 31 East 2nd Street, Mineola, N.Y. 11501

Library of Congress Cataloging-in-Publication Data

Treasury of book ornament and decoration.

(Dover pictorial archive series)
Derived from material originally edited by Cesare Ratta in: L'Arte del libro e della rivista. 1927; and Gli Adornatori del libro in Italia. 1925–1926.
   1. Type ornaments.   2. Book ornamentation.   3. Borders, Ornamental (Decorative arts).   4. Illustration of books—Italy.   5. Printing, Practical—Specimens.   I. Grafton, Carol Belanger.   II. Ratta, Cesare, b. 1857.   III. Arte del libro e della rivista.   IV. Adornatori del libro in Italia.   V. Series.
Z250.3.T72   1986   686.2'24   86-6277
ISBN 0-486-25167-5 (pbk.)

PUBLISHER'S NOTE

Artists and designers desiring a copyright-free ornament or decoration need look no further than this excellent selection of early twentieth-century pictorial materials. Here are decorative initials, representations of books, zodiac signs, musical motifs, animals, people, borders, frames, labels, cartouches and more—all printed on high-quality stock to insure a superior image when used as camera-ready art.

This Dover publication has been derived from material edited by Cesare Ratta in two works: the three-volume set *L'arte del libro e della rivista nei paesi d'Europa e d'America* (The Art of the Book and Magazine in the Nations of Europe and America; at least three variant titles also appear in the publication), published by Ratta in Bologna, 1927, in an edition of only 750 copies; and in Volume III of the three-volume set *Gli adornatori del libro in Italia* (Creators of Book Ornament in Italy), 1925–26, as published by Julius Wisotzki, Chicago (obviously an American imprint for part of the Italian edition). The selection by Carol Belanger Grafton has been made with an eye toward retaining the finest works from the original collection and providing those designs that will best serve the needs of today's artists and designers.

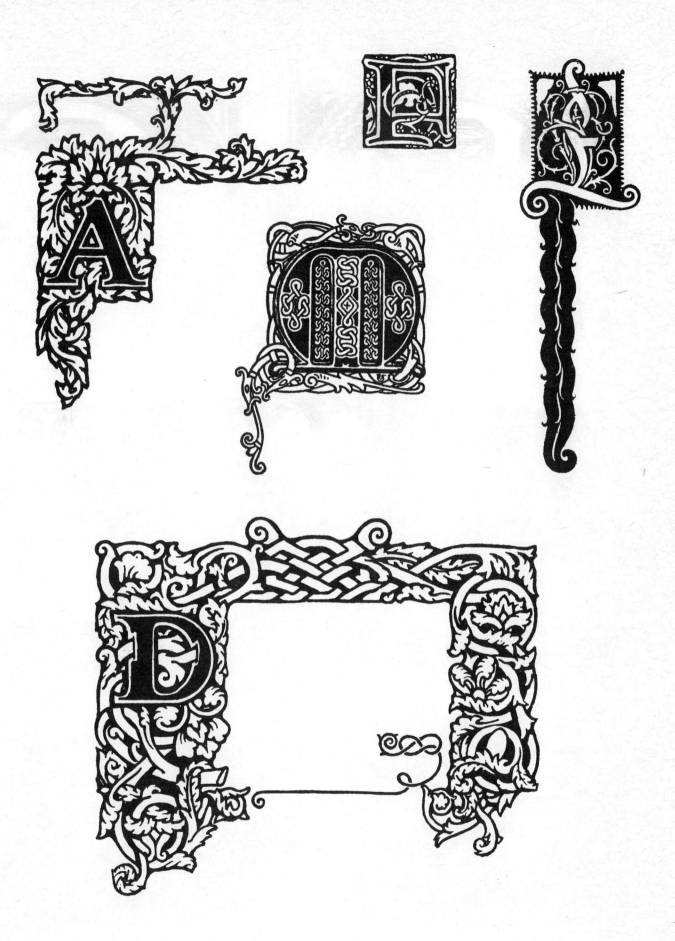

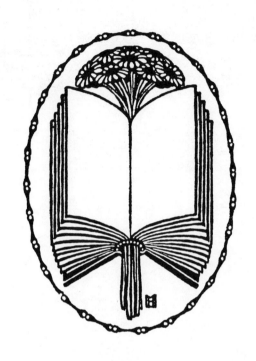

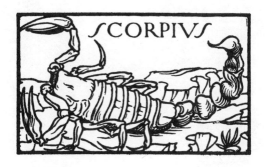

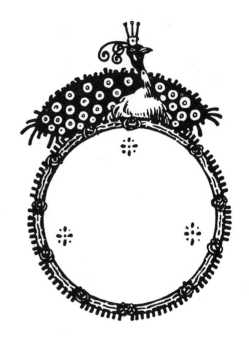

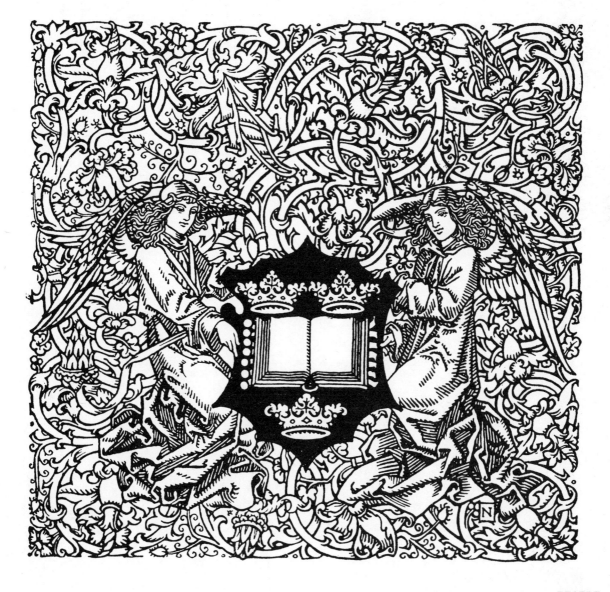

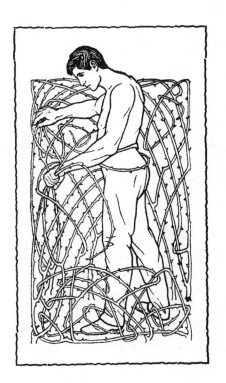

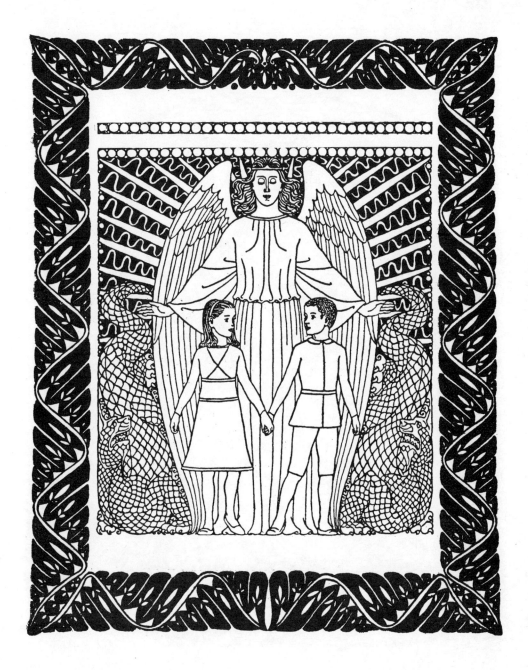

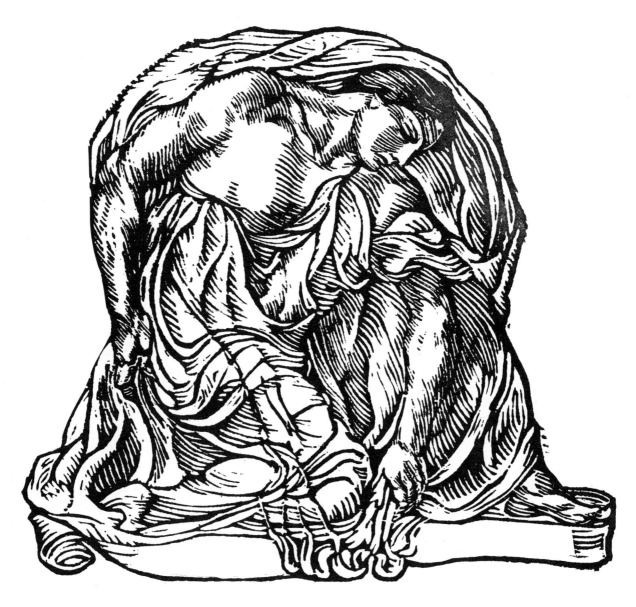

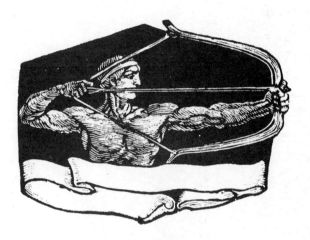

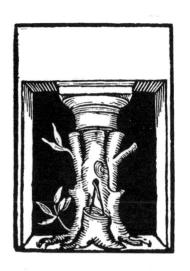

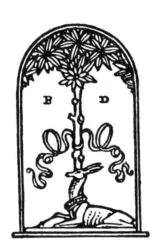

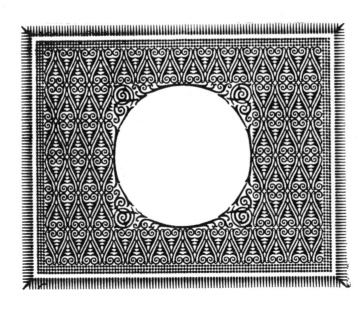

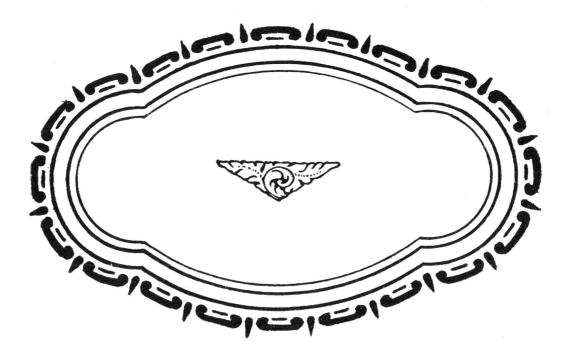

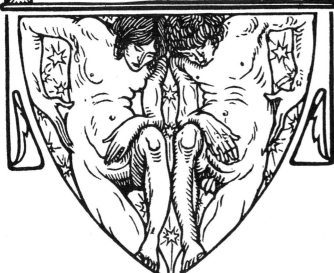

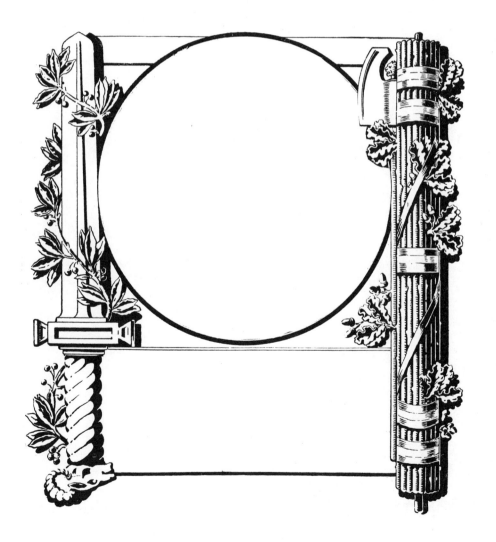

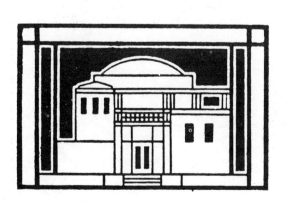

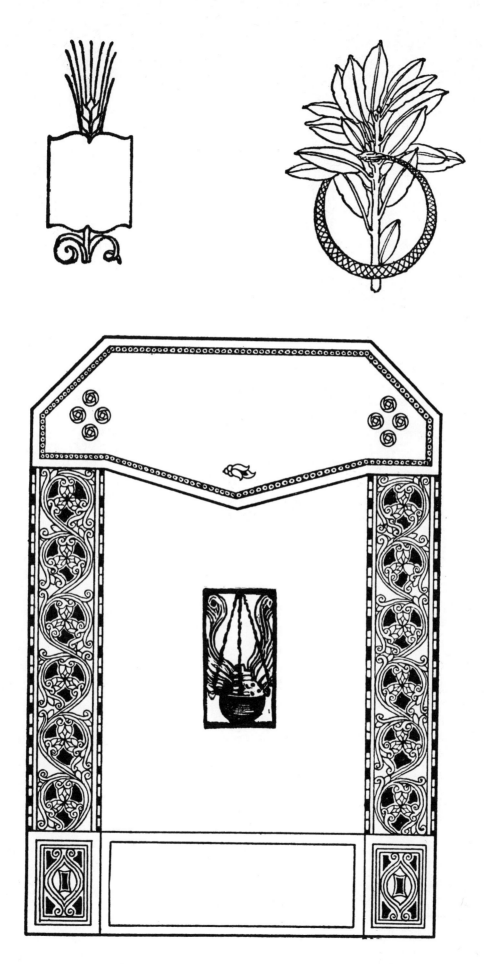

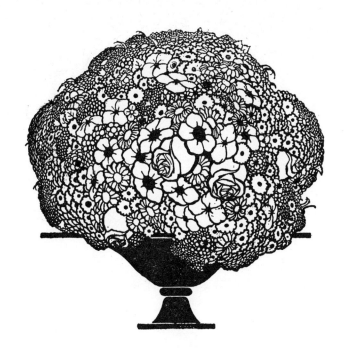

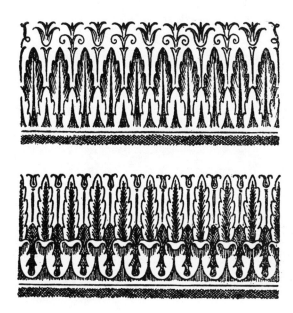
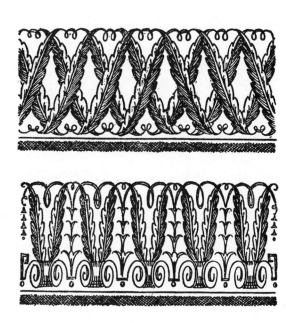

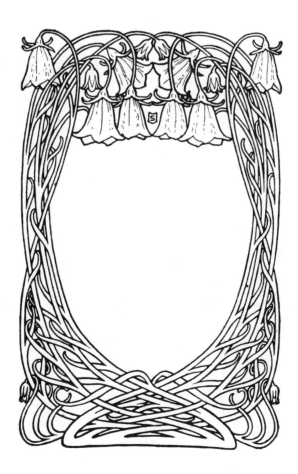

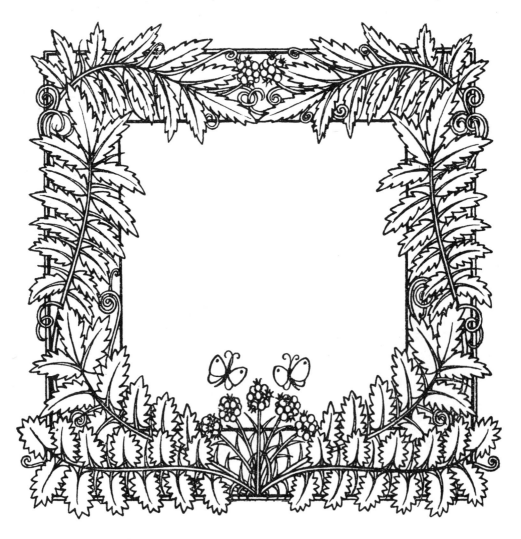

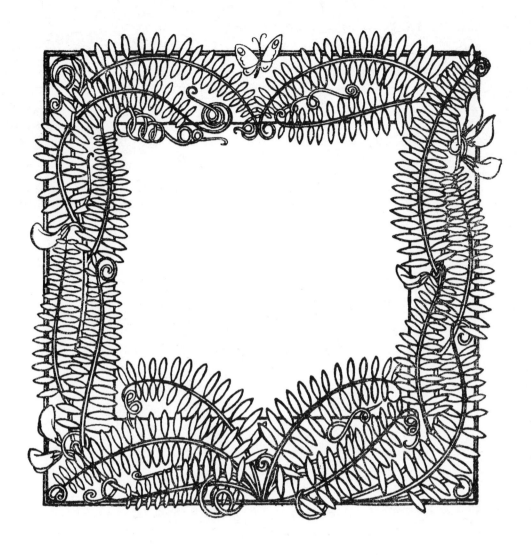

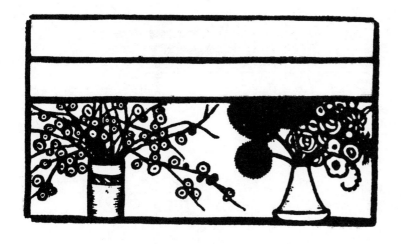

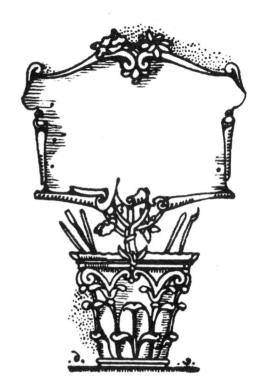